HOW TO PLAY THE UKULELE

HOW TO PLAY THE UKULELE

A Complete Guide for Beginner

DYLAN GREEN

Dylan Green

Contents

How to Play the Ukulele
A Complete Guide for Beginners

WRITTEN BY DYLAN GREEN

Copyright

the pages described forthwith shall be considered both accurate and truthful when it comes to the recounting of facts. As such, any use, correct or incorrect, of the provided information will render the Publisher free of responsibility as to the actions taken outside of their direct purview. Regardless, there are zero scenarios where the original author or the Publisher can be deemed liable in any fashion for any damages or hardships that may result from any of the information discussed herein.

Additionally, the information in the following pages is intended only for informational purposes and should thus be thought of as universal. As befitting its nature, it is presented without assurance regarding its prolonged validity or interim quality. Trademarks that are mentioned are done without written consent and can in no way be considered an endorsement from the trademark holder.

Table of Contents

Introduction

In this guidebook, we are going to spend some time looking at the magical ukulele, and all that it has to offer to the musician. This is an extremely popular instrument, one that is easy to work with and learn how to use, I you are willing to put in the time and effort. Thinking on to some of the relaxing days on the beach of Hawaii, dreaming about the ocean breeze, can help you to come up with images of this instrument, and will help you to really become one with this instrument.

This guidebook is going to take look over how you can learn how to play the ukulele for yourself. We will explore what the ukulele is, some of the cords that you need to learn how to play, and even some of the different parts of this instrument. There are so many things to get started with on this instrument that it may seem a bit overwhelming when you start. But this guidebook will ensure that it is as easy as possible so that you can play some of your favorite songs in no time.

Among electrified and powerful technologically advanced music, the ukulele remains humble and proud of its well-known roots as Hawaii's instrument of choice in the 19th and 20th centuries. This book aims to further the instrument's popularity across the world and bring this amazing instrument into the homes of future songwriters and musicians. When you are ready to learn more about the ukulele and all that it has to offer, make sure to check out this guidebook to help you out!

Chapter 1: The History of the Ukulele

The first thing that we need to take a look at is some of the history of this instrument. When we take the time to know more about the instrument, it is easier to know where it came from, and how it has reached its modern form. This is part of what makes the ukulele so unique. You will find that it is such a great instrument because it has so many journeys and has traveled to so many parts of the world. And each region of the world who has gotten their hands on this instrument have gone through and made it their own.

Let's start back at the beginning. One of the first times that the ukulele was mentioned is found in the Metropolitan Museum of Art's catalog. This catalog would list out a bunch of instruments from around the world and was published in 1902. In fact, in this year, there were two different descriptions about ukulele's that came out of Hawaii. These including the soprano ukulele, and one that looked similar to the tenor that we use today.

Of course, even though this was one of the first times that we saw a ukulele in print doesn't mean that was when it was invented. In fact, in the late 1800s is when the ukulele was invented in Portugal. At the time, this ukulele was developed to look similar to some of the other stringed instruments found in Portugal and Spain, such as the small guitar, but changed to be something unique.

At the time, the guitar was very popular, and was starting to spread out through the Spanish world and more. There are a variety of different guitars that are out there, each with their own unique sound and use. But when it comes to string instruments, the ukulele is going to be one of the most unique, and one of the most fun to play.

So, how did this instrument came from Hawaii? Why do we have visions of sitting near the ocean in Hawaii strumming along to this instrument? It is believed that immigrants from Portugal, mainly from the area of Madeira, came to Hawaii with these ukulele's and would entertain local residents with their sweet music each night. It didn't take long until the King of the islands, who was known as a big supporter of the arts, heard about the ukulele and started inviting musicians to royal gatherings to play. And the popularity with the instrument grew from there.

Since the inhabitants of Hawaii fell in love with the ukulele, it didn't take long until this started to spread to other parts of the world. By the early 1900s, both the United States and Japan started to see more of the ukulele as well. The first time that the ukulele was spotted in the United States was at the Panama-Pacific International Expo. At that Expo, one of the pavilions was from Hawaii, and it included musicians who were able to play both the ukulele and guitar. Many people who attended this Expo fell in love with the ukulele, and this launched how popular it was in America.

The ukulele was able to bring in a new wave of instruments and music throughout America. Along with the steel guitar, which was gaining popularity at the time as well, the ukulele was able to bring about new types of music, was easy to play, and could be taken around with relative ease. It didn't take long until the ukulele started to make its appearance in a variety of musical genres including old time country and jazz.

After World War II, the ukulele actually grew even more, and it was produced in mass. The advent of various technologies for distribution and manufacturing allowed this instrument to be spread around and taught to people throughout the country.

By the 1960s, there was a decline in the use of the ukulele. Thanks to psychedelic music that started during this time, the guitar rose in popularity instead. In fact, the ukulele took such a back seat throughout the years that it wasn't until the 1990s, when the song "Over the Rainbow" by a Hawaiian musician was released before people even remembered what the ukulele was.

If you have ever worked with another string instrument, especially a guitar or something similar, then you already have a good start on how to work with the ukulele you will find that the sound that you will get out of this instrument is going to be a lot different, but the position of the strings and the notes that you are going to play will come in pretty similar.

Even if you have never played another string instrument in the past, learning how to work with the ukulele can be a fun experience. Once you get used to the way tat you need to strum the strings on this instrument, and you learn what each of the notes mean on the sheet music (and where to place your hands in order to get those notes to play on the instrument), you will be able to play any song that you would like.

The history of this instrument may be short and sweet, just like the songs that it is able to play. Songwriters through-out the world love to experiment with the ukulele because it allows them to get a very distinct sound on an instrument that is easy to learn and play. Whether you have played an-other string instrument or not, the ukulele is a great option to implement into your repertoire.

2

Chapter 2: Getting to Know Your Ukulele

So now that we know a bit more about the ukulele and how this instrument works, it is time to learn a bit more about our new friend. Knowing the different parts of this stringed instrument, and how it all goes together can make a big difference in how well you learn to play it.

First, let's look at some of the different types of ukulele's that you can learn how to play. The soprano ukulele is going to be the type that you most likely have because it is the standard size and has the sweetest sound. There are also two other options, the tenor and the baritone. After the soprano comes the tenor, which comes with a louder volume and a deeper bass tone. And finally, we get introduced to the baritone, which is going to be like a small guitar in size, but with a slightly different sound to it.

Tuning

So, the first thing that we need to look at with our ukulele is to make sure that it is tuned property. Tuning the ukulele is going to take some time, and you do need to have a good ear to make this happen. But once the ukulele is tuned properly, you will be able to sit back and enjoy all of the amazing sounds that come from it.

While it is possible that you can change things up and practice with some alternate tunings, as a beginner, you should stick with the standard tuning method. Once you get some more experience with that, you will be able to make some adjustments and change the sound based on what you would like to play. To start with this, you need to know the order of the strings which are, going from the string farthest from you and up is A, E, C, and G.

In order to tune the instrument properly, you need to know how each note is supposed to sound. For those who have played other instruments in the past, it is going to be easy to figure out how to tune the strings of the ukulele, and you will just need to go with the sound that you are used to for these notes.

But the challenge comes in when you have never played the ukulele before at all, or any instrument. Learning the sounds of these notes, either through practice or with the help of a tuner. Both of these will make it so much easier for you to make sure that the ukulele sounds the way that it should through tuning.

If you haven't played and instrument before, and you don't know what those four notes should sound like, then it is best to purchase a tuner to help. These are available from many music shops, or some smartphones have an app that you can use as well. Over time, you will get more familiar with how these notes are meant to sound, and you can do it all by ear, rather than relying on the tuner all the time.

Once you are ready to tune, either with a tuner or by ear, you can grab the ukulele and pluck one of the strings If the string sounds like the note you get from the tuner, then you don't need to do anything more with this. But if not, you will need to turn the string either looser or together to get the right note. So, let's say that you pluck your C string and the tuner reads out that it is sounding like a B note, you will need to make some changes. You can pluck that same string again and tighten the string until it gets to the C note according to your tuner. Make sure to do this process with the other four strings as well before you start to play.

If you are uncertain about how to work on tuning the ukulele, then asking someone to give you some guidance can be the best option possible. They can work wit you to learn how the notes should sound, how much you should turn the strings, and what it takes to get the notes in the right pitch.

Be careful when you are tuning your ukulele. One thing that a lot of beginners run into trouble with is that they are trying to turn the knobs too much, and one of the strings is going to break in the process You only need to turn the strings a little bit in order to get the tune to change a bit. If you turn the knobs too much or too quickly, it is going to result in the string breaking.

It is usually a good idea to keep some extra strings around, just in case. As a beginner, you have to learn how to play and tune the instrument in the proper manner, and until you are able to do this, you may find that you pluck too hard, or you turn the knobs while tuning too hard. Even if you are gentle with the strings, it is likely that, over time, they are going to wear out and you will need to replace them as well

Having an extra string around to deal with these breakages ensures that you can get a new string on right away and get back to playing without any delays.

The body of the instrument

The body is going to be pretty easy to figure out. It is basically just the largest section of your instrument. It will usually be made out of wood and will have a hollow part in it to allow the sound to come out. The size of the ukulele body, and its shape, will help determine the sound that you are able to get out of it. A smaller body means that the sound will be softer and more of a soprano. A bigger body can get the deeper and louder sounds.

Strings

We talked about them a bit above, but all ukuleles are going to have four strings. The strings are going to be made out of nylon, though there are some traditional and unique instruments that have strings made out of different materials. The strings will be either plucked or strummed, which causes them to resonate and create the sound that you hear when they are played.

You won't own the ukulele for long before you notice that the strings take some time to take care of. Over time, especially if you play this instrument a lot, you will find that some of the strings will wear out, and even become dirty. This can change up both the volume and the tone of the instrument and makes it hard to keep this in tune. When you are working on changing these strings, pay attention to the way that they attach to your instrument, so you make sure they go back the right way.

Nut

The next piece of the ukulele that we need to focus on is the nut. This is going to be either a piece of plastic or bone that will help to hold your strings in the right spot. The main role of this is to make sure that the strings stay apart from one another, and that they stay at the right height, so you get the sound that you want.

Tuning keys

When you are working on tuning your strings so they make the right sound, you will utilize the tuning keys at some point. These will be found at the top of the ukulele, at the headstock, and the strings will be wrapped around them a bit. You can turn these keys around to either loosen or tighten the strings to get the write sound. A good way to remember this is that when you tighten the string, the note will get higher. But when you loosen the string, the note will be lower.

You will need to get familiar with these tuning strings. Knowing more about them and how to use them in the proper manner is going to make a difference on how well you are able to play this instrument. Many times you will need to tune the strings to make sure that the right sound comes out of them, or you will want to change the tuning a bit to different sound for a particular song you will get very familiar with these tuning keys as you go.

The neck

When you look at the ukulele, you will see that the long piece between the headstock and the body will be the neck.

The neck is going to be thin and will be easy for you to hold onto when you are playing this instrument. Depending on how long the neck is, you could have fewer or more frets; when the neck is long there are more frets and the shorter it is the fewer frets there are. What this means is that when you have an instrument with more frets, there will be more range between the available high and low notes.

Bridge

The bridge is next on the list. This is going to be usually a piece of wood that is located on the body of this instrument and will have the strings attached to it. The main goal of this bridge is to hold onto the strings as securely as possible to ensure that the tension stays on the strings. If there is no tension found, then you will run into trouble getting the notes to make any sound at all.

The bridge can also have some thin pieces of plastic or bone, like what we see with the nut. These are there to help you keep your strings along the right places, so they stay tuned, and allows for some adjustment in the height of the string if it is needed.

Headstock

Next on the list is going to be the headstock. You will find that this part is found at the end of the instruments neck and will hold onto the tuning keys. You can often find the logo of the brand for this ukulele there as well. The headstock can come in a variety of shapes and is pretty much there to be ornamental.

There are also a number of other parts that you may want to consider for your ukulele to make playing it a bit easier. Some of the other parts that you can consider will include:

- The tuner: This can help you make sure that the strings are at the right pitch to play the notes that you want
- Pick: You can choose to just use your fingers for this or use a pick to make things easier.
- Case: A case can help you to store the ukulele and keep it safe for when it is being transported or stored.
- Stand: Stands are a great option to hold onto the ukulele any time that you are not playing it. You could just hold it against the wall, but this makes it more likely that the instrument is going to fall down and become broken in the process.
- Cleaning accessories: At some point, your ukulele is going to get dirty, whether from storage or use. Picking out a few safe products to clean the product with can help to keep it in good working order.
- Strap: Since the ukulele is a bit smaller than some of the other instruments available, you may be fine just holding onto it. But some musicians choose to have a strap with this to make it easier to hold onto and use.

These are the basic parts of your ukulele. Take a moment to look for all of them on the instrument to determine where they are and how you would use them. Even though there are a few different types of ukuleles out there for you to use, they all will come with the same kinds of parts that you will need to become familiar with.

3

Chapter 3: Playing Styles and Techniques

Once you are familiar with your ukulele and how it works, it is time to learn a bit about how to play this instrument. There are a lot of different parts that come with the ukulele, and understanding how it works, and even how to hold the instrument, can make a difference in the way that you are able to play. Let's explore some of the different ways to play the ukulele, and the different techniques that you can use to go from beginner to professional in no time.

How do I hold the ukulele?

When it comes to playing this instrument, you will need to be able to stay in the same holding position for a bit of time. Because of this, you want to be careful to sit or stand in a way that will allow you to maintain this posture, at least for the amount of time that you are playing. The most important thing to consider is how comfortable your arm and hand is during this time. if your hands get cramped or hurt during this time, then it is hard for you to play and enjoy yourself.

Some people find that they are the most comfortable when they sit down and place this allows them to set the ukulele down a little bit, so they aren't straining as much. You need to figure out what seems to be the most comfortable for you, and then go with that option. This allows you to get the songs to sound great, without being uncomfortable at the same time

Another thing to consider is to give your hands some stretching before you start playing, especially if you plan to play for a long time. You can also mess around with the instrument a bit and see how it feels, whether you want to change up a few things here and there, and just make sure that it is ready to go.

There are many different stretching exercises that you can do with your hands. Practicing your scales or doing a few easy songs right when you first get started is a great way to help you to make those fingers stronger, and to ensure they are nice and warmed up before you decide to start playing at all.

Playing with the strings

The first technique that we are going to look at is striking the strings. There are actually more than one method that you can use in order to get the string to make a noise. These are often going to be split up between either picking or strumming, but in these categories, there is a lot of variation.

To start, we need to take a look at strumming. This is when you will move your fingers so that more than one string resonates at the same time. Picking, on the other hand is when you just do one string at a time. There are a few different techniques that you can use that will fit into each of these categories, but as a beginner, we are going to just take a look at the general idea that comes with these.

One thing to remember here is that when you decide to strike a string, the harder that you do this, the louder the sound will be, and the longer that sound will last. If you want it to be a softer sound from the string, then make sure that you pluck gently. But if you want a loud and that resonates and lasts for a bit, then you need to pluck the string a little bit harder. One of the things that you should experiment as you learn some music is how to alternate between soft and hart plucking so that you can add your own personal style when playing.

Strumming

Strumming is one of the methods that you can use when you start to play the ukulele. The most common way to do this is to take all four of the strings and strum them together at the same time. using either the tip of your index finger or your thumb is the best way to make this happen. You can seem awkward, but a bit of practice is going to make it work a bit better.

Strumming your way down the strings, and then going back up again, and repeating in this manner will help you to get a nice rhythm that is constant and can work well for this. This method can also help you to mute some of your strings as well if you choose. You can strum a bit and then stop the strings using your hand, placing it on the fretboard, so that it sounds more like a percussion sound and adding in a beat to the string instrument if you choose.

There will be times when you work with chords while playing this instrument. Chords that are made up of a lot of different notes can be more difficult to work with and can add in a bit of complexity to your song. Being able to strum in this manner helps you to add in these beautiful chords, without needing a lot of practice.

We will take some time to show you different chords that you are able to strum, and you will get better at doing it throughout some time and practice. Many times, we will find that it is easier to pluck when we learn, but there is so much more that you can do with strumming, especially when it comes to your personal style and some of the music you choose to play.

Picking

The other common style of striking the strings is picking. Unlike the guitar which many musicians who use it will like to use their fingers to pluck at the strings. But there is some freedom to the method that you choose. Another option is to use a pick the strings. This is sometimes faster than the other options and you won't have to worry about your fingers getting stuck. ,

One fingerpicking style commonly referred to as finger-style. This style means that you are going to use your thumb to play the bass line. At the same time, you are going to play the method as well. An expert who has had a lot of practice with this will actually be able to make the ukulele sound like more than one instrument at the same time.

Playing lead is pretty straight forward. You play single notes, often the melody, while other instruments keep a rhythm. This allows the player to showcase their melodic playing and picking prowess. Typically performed with backing members of a band or utilizing technology and looping the rhythm then playing your lead over the recorded rhythm.

When striking the strings, there are many ways to go about it. It is recommended that you practice all techniques throughout your ukulele career, but naturally some styles are more appealing than others, and it just feels right to pursue what comes naturally. Practice picking with four fingers each one assigned to a certain string. Simply practicing your attack on the strings will help keep the fingers limber and assist in exploring different picking patterns.

The strumming and picking patterns are very important to your particular style; no one person picks or even strums a ukulele exactly the same as anyone else, so be creative and comfortable with your playing style. If you feel like strumming with your thumb is uncomfortable then use your index finger. Being open-minded and allowing yourself to grow and learn the way that you prefer is a big part of how music can be a personal healing and learning experience.

Both the strumming and the picking patterns can help you to play a lot of the songs that you are looking for. But they are both very different techniques and can often give a different vibe to the song. It is often best if you are able to learn how to make both of these methods work so that you can learn how to use them for any song that you want to play.

With a little strumming and picking practice down we can now move on to the language of music theory.

4

Chapter 4: Music Theory

Music theory is an organized study of music. There are set guidelines and a language that is used to organize the expansive musical universe. These guidelines allow musicians to communicate with each other and interpret songs and other compositions. This language is our best attempt to tame and immerse ourselves in the study of music. While music at its roots is very chaotic and hard to contain, this musical language was created by humanity to understand the sounds better and understand each other. Let's explore some of the language and keywords you need to know.

Notes

Another part that we need to focus on here are the notes. The whole foundation of the chords and the scales that we will look at in this guidebook will be notes. Without knowing the notes, you will never be able to play any of your favorite songs, or make up some of your own.

To keep it simple, the notes are going to be the individual sounds that are given a name, which is a letter ranging from A to G in the alphabet. You will be able to recognize these notes by the pitch they have; each note has its own pitch that distinguishes it from all the others. You can augment these pitches, which means that you go up just half a step above the note. Or you can diminish it, which means that you will go lower by half a step. The pitch of these notes can be sharp or flat as well. You will know that the note is flat when you get a little lower pitch. But you can tell when the note is sharp when it has a higher pitch.

The pitch

We talked about pitch a bit above, but it is still something that we need to take the time to look at here. Pitch is going to basically be the rate that the vibration goes for the sound of a note. You will either have a high pitch, or a low pitch, depending on the note that you are working with. Pitch is pretty easy to work with. When the vibration is faster, then the pitch is going to be higher. But the opposite is true as well. When the vibration is slower on the strings, this means that the pitch is lower.

Intervals

There is a distance that occurs between the two notes that you are playing on the ukulele. This distance is going to be known as the interval. These intervals are usually measured by half steps and these half steps are going to be known as a semi-tone. These intervals can be important because they are going to be the part that helps to create the melodies that you play. And when you play notes at the same time, you will be playing a chord. But playing notes one at a time means you are playing a scale.

Scales

Scales are notes that have been placed together, in a certain order, for you to play individual notes. If you notice that the pitch of all the notes that you are playing is going up, then this is something known as an ascending scale. On the other side, if you see that the pitch is going down, then this means you are playing a descending scale.

There are a lot of different scales that you can play on this instrument. When you play them though, this is the time when you will strike the notes all on their own, one at a time, rather than doing them all together to make a chord. While there are a few different scales that you can work with to make music, you will typically go from one note, up to the same note that is higher, or the same note that is lower. The difference that comes between these scales is going to be known as a scale step.

Are there different scale types?

When it comes to scales, they are going to be listed out based on the number of pitches that are inside of them. Some of the scale names that you will encounter when working with this will include:

1. **Monotonic**: These scales are going to have one note.
2. **Diatonic**: These scales are going to have two notes in them.
3. **Tritonic**: These are going to include three notes in them.
4. **Tetratonic**: These scales are going to have four notes in them.

5. **Pentatonic**: These scales are going to include five notes in them.

6. **Hexatonic**: These scales are going to include 6 notes in them.

7. **Heptatonic**: These scales are going to include 7 notes in them.

8. **Octatonic**: These scales are going to include eight notes in them.

9. **Chromatic**: These scales are going to have twelve notes per octave.

These scales are going to be listed out with any kind of key that you want to use in the music. The nice thing about this is that they will make sure that your song has a distinct character, and some new personality into the song. And when you start a new song, you will have a scale position that they like to stick with.

Chords

Chords are combinations of various notes played at the same time. The starting note is considered a root note. Not unlike scales, the two main types are major and minor. There is more information on chords and a chord chart later in the book. Chords often require the player to be pressing all the strings at once in any given position, but many major and minor chords have 'open' strings as well. An open string is a string that is played without being pressed against the fretboard by the player.

The structures of the chords

Before you every start to work on a song, you need to learn the basics of chords. The shape, as well as the structure, of these chords can be helpful when you want to play any kind of string instrument. A chord is going to contain at least two notes, but usually more, that are played at the same time. in most of the songs that you want to work with, there will be many chords that are strung together to get the song that you recognize.

When you are starting to learn some of the chord shapes, you need to remember that any shape of the chords can be moved around on the fretboard. The example that we are going to have below will help you to learn the shape of the chords, before we even have time to learn the steps to reading music!

To start, we need to look at the basic chord types that you can work with. There are four basic chord types, and these include:

1. **The major chords**: These chords are the ones that will contain both the major third, as well as the major fifth notes.
2. **The minor chords**: These are almost the same as the ones above. But instead of having the major third and fifth notes, they are going to have the minor ones.
3. **Diminished chords**: These will have a combination of the minor third note and then it will go together with the diminished fifth.
4. **Augmented chords**: This one is the opposite of the

diminished chords. It will have an augmented fifth and a major third.

5. **Seventh chords**: These are going to contain any of the notes that we talked about above. But then you will add in a seventh note to the mix as well.

These are just a few of the chord types that you can work with. But many times, the chords can get complex, and the ones above are going to be a good starting point for those who are beginners.

From here, there are going to be chord progressions. These are going to be a series of chords that will be organized in a way that will create a nice melody for you to use. These can technically be any chords that you want, but usually you want to go with ones that are the most pleasing to the ear when you put them together. But then, once you learn how to put these chords together, you may find that adding some eerie chords, or something that sounds a bit off, can add in a unique sound to your music.

Understanding the timing of a song

Any time that you play any song, no matter what kind of music you are working with, or what instrument, there has to be musical timing. When you are considered in time, it means that you are playing the song in a consistent rhythm compared to any other instruments playing, or with the music on it's own.

Tempo is part of this time, and that is going to be the speed at which you play the music. When the tempo is set, you will usually keep it the same from the start of the song until it is all over. Tempo is very important. It can help you to express different emotions in the song. Slow tempos will help you feel differently about a song than one that is set at a faster tempo.

When you look at a sheet of music, you will notice that it has a time signature that is set up on there. This is going to be the number of beats per measure of a song. There are different time signatures that you can see, but for many songs, especially those for beginners, the time signature is going to be 4/4. This means that there are four peats per measure, and four measures per bar. This is a pretty steady beat and is easier for beginners to learn.

Song Structure

The structure of songs is comprised of many different sections. Versus, choruses, bridges, reprises, and many other musical terms comprise the different sections. There are no specific rules when it comes to songwriting, but many writers pride themselves on creating complex chord structures and melodies. It is important to value simplicity as well when it comes to songs. Some of the most powerful music is made up of simple arrangements. So, approach songs and songwriting with an open mind.

Below I will provide you with some basic definitions of song structure terms. Although many songs adhere to a basic structure, you can get outside the box, or experimental, and create songs that are all your own.

There are many parts that can come with a song. It is important to know these parts because they may change up the chords that you are using, and other things that you need to do while playing. Some of the most common types of sections found in a song include:

1. **The verse**: This is going to be similar to a stanza in a poem. It is going to contain a rhyming structure that you can find repeated more than one time in the song. This is often the story, as well as the heart, that you see in the song itself. You will find that these parts are going to catch the attention of the listener, and they can be like the personality.

2. **Chorus**: When we look at the chorus, we are going to look at the part of the song that repeats itself more than once in the song. They may have a lyric that is easy to remember or a nice melody. And if you are working with a popular song and learning how to play it, then it most likely has the name of the song in it.

3. **Bridge**: This is more of a transition in the song. It can help to either break up a repetitive song, or to connect together different parts. It will break away from some of the structure that you saw in the rest of the song, before heading back into the chorus.

4. **Outro**: Another thing to consider is the outro, which is also known as the ending of that song. Sometimes it will be similar to the intro, or it may just be the chorus. If it is a recording of the song, this outro can fade into the ending of the song.

5. **Arrangement**: This is going to be any reworking of a song that was written in the past. For example, newer artists may take an older folk song, where the writer

isn't known, and then arrange it into a newer song for them to use.

6. **The lyrics**: This one is something that many musicians, and non-musicians, know about. It is going to be the words that come with a song. There are going to be some songs that don't have these lyrics. But the lyrics can help tell a story with the song.

7. **Instrumental or the solo**: There are some songs where the lyrics will stop and then it is just the instrument playing. If there are many instruments playing, this solo will let one instrument be the lead so that a player can show off their skills.

Knowing the different parts that come with a song will make it a bit easier. It will ensure that you know what is going on with the song, that you are prepared to deal with the different parts as you play. You will find yourself more prepared for the chord changes that can happen in the different parts of the song. And when it is time to write some of your own songs, you will find that knowing these different parts will make that a whole lot easier.

5

Chapter 5: Understanding Chord Charts and How They Can Help with Reading Music

Even as a beginner, it is easy to learn the different shapes of the chords that you will work with. When you do these chords, you have to remember that the strings don't need to have an assigned fret that is played open unless it is noted in other ways. When we are working with these chord shapes, you need to remember that moving the shape so that it goes up or down the fretboard means that you will need to make sure that the notes are up also. This can be done with the index finger so that the bar chord is formed, and then the problem is solved.

The charts that we have in this chapter will show us the chords that you can use with the ukulele. When you see the red dots on there, this is the place where you need to put the finger on the string. Then there will be an area with a straight line, and then some dots that go over the whole picture. In these areas, you will need to bar a chord, which will need the use of your index finger to finish. To help with this pictures, imagine that you are holding onto the ukulele, and you are looking right so that the fretboard is at you. So, on these charts, the top string will be on the bottom from your perspective of looking at the ukulele.

The chords below will be a good place for you to start. Practice them a bit now because you will be able to use them in some of the songs that we have prepared at the end of this guidebook. Another thing to spend some time looking at is the notes that come with each of these chords. This can make it easier for you to see the relationship between the scales and the chords.

After you have had some time to look over these chords and you have a good idea of how they work and you may be able to work on them from memorization. Don't feel bad if you need some more practice. This is a great way for you to learn a little bit more about how to play the ukulele, can help you to get comfortable, and helps your fingers to move along as well.

With the abundance of chords when it comes to music, it can seem overwhelming, but do not be discouraged. Some of the most influential songs in popular music history are composed of only major or minor chords. As you learn to play more melodically, you will need to become familiar with more chords that are considered complex so that you are able to get the song and the melody that is so important to you. With some of these chords, you may try them out and notice that they are a bit strange sounding as first, mostly because of the notes you use, or the way you place the fingers. But many of these are going to be chords that you will quickly become familiar with as you get more experience.

With all these things in mind and a little bit of chord practice under our belts let's move on to the song portion of the book. Following this chapter will be a list of popular songs ready to play. Let's get ready!**Chapter 6: Songs**

6

Chapter 6: Songs

Now that you know a little bit more about the ukulele and some of the different chords that come with this instrument, it is time to add in a few songs that you can practice and learn. The songs below have the chords printed out without lyrics because we are not allowed to use the lyrics since they are copywritten. Listen to these songs—unless you already know them—and play along with the tracks you find on YouTube or other online resources. As you practice, the songs will become easier to memorize—and eventually, you will be able to play them by heart. Even if you're not a singer, playing along and singing for practice is a great way to learn about timing and how to keep it consistent. By synchronizing the lyrics and the chords, you allow the timing, chords, and lyrics to really come together and create the song.

Practicing picking the melody of the lyrics is a great exercise as well. The songs below should be familiar to you, but if they're not, you can go online and find versions of them to listen to—this is a great exercise as well—and playing along with already recorded songs will help you with timing and style. Keep in mind that some songs you find online may be in a different key than the keys listed below—we have tried to choose the most common key for the songs.

Although playing along with already recorded songs is a great way for you to learn some songs and get a bit of practice in with the ukulele. You can then go through and change it up to match some of the personal style that you want. This is also known as a cover song. When covering a song, you typically keep the lyrics and chord progressions but change the tempo or key. Also, as you may know, the songs below don't use ukuleles on the original tracks—so even by playing it in the ukulele, you have transformed the song and created a decent cover song.

Even without going with the lyrics that we will present to you later on in this guidebook, you can simply go through and strum some of the chords that are listed and understand and hear a song that is familiar to you. This is the neat thing about music. You will be able to hear the music of the song, without even needing to hear the lyrics.

The chords that you will create with the instrument and your fingers will give you a melody the chords together, rather than doing the notes individually. As you look at the chords and strum along with the notes that you see, you may even get so into the music that you are able to start humming and singing the song on your own.

Of course, even with a song that you know well, there are going to be parts that will stop you and parts that will be difficult. The songs you know can be easier since you know what to expect, but some of the arrangements, the transitions, and more can miss you up. Don't let this discourage you though. Just keep practicing and you will be able to play the song without any issues.

As you begin with the songs below, keep in mind there are millions of songs out there—if you don't like the songs listed below, there are plenty of websites and songbooks that focus on genres and styles. Feel free to adventure out and find songs that really resonate with you. Finding a style and feel that you prefer is ideal to the musician, it is his/her personality that comes through the music. With all the different styles and genres out there, along with the versatility of the ukulele, you can surely find a sound that you love, or maybe create your own!

Having an arsenal of songs that you have memorized is an excellent way to show off your newfound skills as a ukulele player. Learning a song all the way through is rewarding and fun. The sense of accomplishment after learning multiple songs gives you the confidence to create your own songs and draw inspiration from your personal repertoire. The combination of playing cover songs and your own original ones makes for a great practice of comparison. After composing a few songs, you learn that the art of composition is a brutally honest one. You may hate your songs, but other people love them. Some songs age well while others are perfect right off the bat. Below I will share some tips on writing original songs and some simple techniques to write with.

Amazing Grace

FF

C7

FF7BbF

DmC7FBb/C

FBbF

C7

FF7BbF

DmC7FD7

GCG

GD

GG7CG

EmDGC/D

GC G

GD7

GG7CG

EmDGE

ADA

E7

AA7DA

F#mE7F#mD

BED/AA

Over the Rainbow

-Intro-
GDEmC
GDEmEm7C
GD
CG

CG
DEmC
GD
CG

CG
DEmC
G
DEmC
G
D
EmC
GD
CG
CG
DEmC
G
DEmC
G
D
EmC

GD
CG

CG
DEmC

I'm Yours

-Intro-
CGAmF
C
G
Am
F
CG
Am

F
D_7/F#
CGAm
FC
GAm
F
CG
Am
F
CG
Am
F
D_7/F#
CGAm
F
CG
Am
F

CG/BAmG

F

D7/F#

-Instrumental-

CG/BAmGFD7/F#

C

G

Am

F

C

G

Am

F

CGAm

F

CG

Am

F

C

G

Am

FD7CGAmF

What a Wonderful World

CEmFEm
Dm7CE7Am
AbDm7/G
G7CC+F
CEmFEm
Dm7CE7Am
AbDm7/G
G7CFC
G7C
G7 C
AmG/BAm/CG/C
Am/CC#dimDmC#dimG7
CEmFEm
Dm7CE7Am
AbDm7/G
G7CC7
AbDm7/G
G7CAbDm7/GG7C

While My Guitar Gently Weeps

AmAm7Am6Fmaj7

AmGDE

AmAm7Am6Fmaj7

AmGCE

AC#mF#mC#m

BmE

AC#mF#mC#m

BmE

AmAm7Am6Fmaj7

AmGDE

AmAm7Am6Fmaj7

AmGCE

AC#mF#mC#m

BmE

AC#mF#mC#m

BmE

AmAm7Am6Fmaj7

AmGDE

AmAm7Am6Fmaj7

AmGCE

Banana Pancakes

Am

G

D7

GD7

AmC7

GD7

AmC7

GD7

AmC7

GD7

AmC7

Am

G

Am

G

D7

GD7AmC7

GD7AmC7

GD7AmC7

GD7AmC7

Am

G

Am

G

Am

G

Am

G

AmD

AmD

Bm

EmC

GD

G

D7

GD7

AmC7

GD7

D7

AmC7

GD7

AmC7

Am

G

Am

G

Am

G

Am

G

Hey Soul Sister

CGAmF

CG AmF

CGAmFG

CGAmF

CGAmFG

FGCGF

GCG

FGCGFG

CGAmF

CGAmF

CGAmFG

CGAmF

CGAm

FG

FGCGF

GCG

FGCGFG

C

C

GAm

F C

G

Am

FG

FGCGF

GCG

FGCGFGCG
FGCGFG
CGAmFG
CGAmFG
C

CF
AmG
CF
CGC
FA7
DmBbmF
C
FC
CF
AmG
CF
CGC

CF
AmG
CF
CGC
FA7
DmBbmF
C
FC
CF
AmG
CF
CGC
CF
AmG

CF
CGC
FA7
DmBbmF
C
F

Stay with Me

-Intro-
CFCFDmC
AmFC
FDmC
AmFC
F DmC
AmFC
AmFC
GAmFC
AbAmFC
AmFC
AmFC
AmFC
Am GC
AmFC
AmFC
GAmFC
AbAmFC
AmFC
AmFC
GAmFC
AbAmFC
AmFC
AmFC
GAmFC
EAmFC
AmFC

AmFC
GAmFC
AbAmFC

-Intro-
Am G C
Am G C
AmGC
AmGC
AmGC
AmGC
AmGC
AmGC
AmGC
AmGC
AmGC
AmGC
AmGC
AmGC
AmGC
AmGC
AmGC
AmGC
AmGC
AmGC
AmGC
AmG
CF
AmG
CF

AmGC

AmGC

AmGC

AmGC

AmGC

AmGC

AmGC

AmGC

AmGC

AmGC

AmGC

AmGC

AmGC

AmGC

AmGC

Someone Like You

GGmaj7
EmC
GGmaj7
EmC
GGmaj7
EmC
Bm7Em
Am7
Bm7Em
Cmaj7Bm7 Cmaj7
GDEmC
GDEmC
GBm7EmC
GDEmC
GDEmC
GGmaj7
EmC
GGmaj7
EmC
Bm7Em
Am7
Bm7Em
Am7Bm7 Cmaj7 Bm7
GDEmC
GDEmC
GBm7EmC
GDEmC

Gmaj7

Em

Gmaj7Am7Bm7C

GDEmC

GDEmC

GBm7EmC

GDEmC

GDEmC

GDEmC

GBm7EmC

GDEmC

GDEmC

Songwriting Tips

As a beginner to working with the ukulele, there are going to be a few tips that you are able to follow in order to see the results. First, when you are working on making some of your own original songs, you may feel like there is an overwhelming amount of stuff that you need to concentrate on. This is why it is such a great thing to focus on other songs, ones that you know really well, first. You can practice the chords, see what sounds nice, and then be able to translate that over to your own songs.

Once you have gained some practice with other songs, and you feel pretty confident in your abilities to play with the ukulele, it is time to start writing your own songs. This can be pretty simple. Many of the best songs that you love today were started by the musician just grabbing an instrument and playing it, seeing what comes up in the process.

This can be a bit scary for someone who is new to the instrument. Going from playing the chords and notes found on a sheet of paper to making up your own songs can be a big challenge. But this is where your intuition is going to come into play. It will require you to be focused and have some improvisation to succeed.

The good news is that there are a few different steps that you can take in order to create some of your own songs. First, consider the topic, emotion, or more, that you would like to create a song about. Even if you just plan to write out the notes, and not come up with lyrics, there should be some expression with that song. This helps you to keep on track when you write.

If you want to tie an emotion to the song, whether it is sadness or happiness, then the tone and the notes that you pick from should be able to show that to the listener. From there, you will have a lot of freedom here. For example, if you want to talk about a great meal that you just had, but you want it to be heartfelt, there are no rules against doing that. You can write the song about anything that you would like, but have the topic and the tone picked out ahead of time.

After you have worked on the tone, and have a few ideas of chords and tempo that you want to use, now it is time to bring in the lyrics. Not all songs are going to have lyrics to them, so if you don't have any ideas for words, you can skip this part. But writing out the lyrics, and getting an idea of how long the song will be, and how many notes need to be in the intro, verse, chorus and more, will make writing the song easier later one.

Take some time to really write out the words that you would like to have here. Think about whether you would like them to be heartfelt, maybe add in some rhyming, some metaphors, or anything else. Of course, if you just want to write, and not have any grammar tricks in there, that is acceptable as well. This is your song, make it exactly how you want.

Once the lyrics are written down, it is time to work on making the original music that will go with it. You can think through some of the chords that are in your mind when working on the song, or you can grab the instrument and start playing until something sounds right with the lyrics. You can mess around with this one a bit and see what grabs your attention. Then, after getting a few chords together, write them down so that you don't forget.

You can also think deeply about a piece, hear it in your head, and try to recreate it with the ukulele. This practice is a little more difficult but makes for a great mind exercise not to mention a challenging exercise in playing the music itself. The music is going to be the most powerful part of most songs—it creates the mood and offers context for any lyrics that may be in the song. Sometimes there are no words to describe an intense emotion, and that's where music makes its biggest impact.

Record the music. Most smartphones have recording capabilities. Recording yourself and listening back gives a lot of insight into how other people will hear your music. You can even record your song and play along with yourself for practice. If you wish you can purchase recording gear or programs for your computer to make for a more detailed recording process, but most smartphones have recording capabilities built in. By listening back to your recordings, you can almost get an outsiders' perspective on your own music. This allows you to critique the songs and maybe change some parts that you find to be troublesome as you listen back.

Collaborate. Getting together with other musicians or writers offers a unique songwriting experience. Having other people's insight and ideas broadens the spectrum of what the song can become. Sharing music, sharing lyrics, and overall letting the music mold itself into a distinct sound will only expand your musical horizon. Collaboration is also a great way to practice selflessness. Being open-minded as someone suggests that your song needs this or that is a big part of collaborating. Being honest with your collaborators and with yourself is very important in the songwriting process. Be humble when people compliment your music, and be understanding if someone has suggestions for your music.

Composing original music is one of the greatest gifts a musician can offer to their community and the world. Be aware of what you are constructing and make good use of your time as you trek through the world of musical composition and practice. The process truly is magical and has the potential power to change the world at any given time. If there's one bit of advice to give, it is to be joyful and honest in your music.

Composing music is going to be a big deal. It takes a lot of time and effort, and it usually isn't as easy as it may seem. You may go through a lot of different revisions of the song in order to get it to work the way that you want. Don't et this frustrate you. This is completely normal, especially if you are a beginner in the world of playing the ukulele or if you have never played an instrument before.

Sometimes, taking it slowly and learning more about the instrument, and how it works, will ensure that you are going to be able to write some of the best music possible. Rushing in to make sure that you will be able to write music from the beginning, after only knowing a few notes and never playing the instrument before, can cause a lot of issues along the way. you aren't giving yourself time to really know the instrument, or know what it is all about, and this is going to result in a lot of issues, and can make song writing a bit pain to deal with.

If you slow this down, and make sure that you really get to know more about the instrument by playing it for some time, you will become more adept at making your own songs. And, when you are messing around with the music and learning how to play it, you may experiment a bit with the chords and the strings, and be able to make something unique.

While it is an admirable goal to learn how to play a new instrument, and the ukulele is one of the best ones to learn how to use, it is something that is going to take some time and effort as well. Taking the time to really learn how to work with the instrument, and to enjoy playing it for some time is going to make this a lot easier.

Conclusion

Thank you for making it through to the end of *How to Play the Ukulele*! Let's hope it was informative and able to provide you with all the necessary information needed to begin your ukulele journey.

The next step on your journey is to play, play, play, and play! The more time you spend with your instrument, the better. Whether you're practicing popular songs or simply practicing chords over and over, the more you play, the more experience points you get. Practice switching between chords, playing chords, then running scales—and eventually, seek out other musicians to play with if you so choose. Playing in public is a great milestone to achieve, whether it is through an open mic or family dinner. Even if you're not trying to become a professional musician, playing in public feels great and is good for building your relationship with your ukulele.

There are a lot of different instruments out there that you can learn how to play. Some are going to be stringed instruments, some will be loud, some will be quiet, and some will even be unique. But none compare to the ukulele when it comes to the versatility, the ease of learning how to use, and the amazing sound.

This guidebook took some time to talk about the basics of the ukulele, and to ensure that you were able to learn the different parts, some of the different notes that go into the chords of this music, and so much more. We even spent some time seeing a bit of music so that you can get some practice in. as a beginner, you should be set to really use this to your advantage to build up your skills, and your confidence, into the future.

9 782994 820000